B. Strings and Piano

I. *Sonatas*

   (a) *Violin*

1. D major	384	137.1	1816	1836	VIII. 2	54
2. A minor	385	137.2	1816	1836	VIII. 3	54
3. G minor	408	137.3	1816	1836	VIII. 4	54
4. A major	574	162	1817	1851	VIII. 6	54

   (b) *Arpeggione*

A minor	821	—	1824	1871	VIII. 8	56

II. *Other forms* (violin)

1. *Rondeau brillant*, B minor	895	70	1826	1827	VIII. 1	55
2. Fantasy, C major	934	159	1827	1850	VIII. 5	55

III. *Trios*

1. Sonata movement, B♭ major	28	—	1812	1923[5]	—	47
2. B♭ major	898	99	1826	1836	VII. 3	48
3. Nocturne, E♭ major	897	148	1826	1845	VII. 5	47
4. E♭ major	929	100	1827	1828	VII. 4	50

IV. *Quartet*

Adagio and Rondo concertante, F major	487	—	1816	1866	VII. 2	47

V. *Quintet*

A major	667	114	1819	1829	VII. 1	6

C. Wind

1. Octet, F major (Minuet and Finale)	72	—	1813	1889	III. 2	18
2. Eine kleine Trauermusik, E minor (nonet)	79	—	1813	1889	III. 3	18

D. Wind and Strings

Octet, F major	803	166	1824	1853[6]	III. 1	13

E. Wind and Piano

Introduction and Variations, E minor (flute)	802	160	1824	1850	VIII. 7	57

[5] Ed. by Alfred Orel (Wiener Philharmonischer Verlag, Vienna, 1923).
[6] Incomplete edition. First complete edition in G.A.

BBC MUSIC GUIDES

———

SCHUBERT CHAMBER MUSIC

BBC MUSIC GUIDES

Schubert Chamber Music

J. A. WESTRUP

BRITISH BROADCASTING CORPORATION

Published by the British Broadcasting Corporation
35 Marylebone High Street, London W1M 4AA

SBN: 563 08456 1

First published 1969

© J. A. Westrup 1969

Printed in England by
Billing & Sons Limited, Guildford and London

Schubert – Chamber Music

'His character', said Mayrhofer of Schubert, 'was a mixture of tenderness and coarseness, sensuality and candour, sociability and melancholy.' It is a frank opinion, which deserves consideration because it was written by a friend – a friend who knew himself what melancholy meant. It is hardly surprising that it does not agree with the legendary picture of the composer as an innocent child of nature, carelessly singing all day and every day like the grasshopper in the fable. Like every genuine musician Schubert had the gift of intuition, but he was also an enormously hard worker, taking great pains to satisfy himself and to win a reputation; and like most of us he alternated between merriment and gloom. That he was to a large extent unsuccessful in the worldly sense was due in part to the fact that he never held any official position: and unlike Beethoven he was not supported by aristocratic patrons. His friends were men with sympathies akin to his own – painters, poets and fellow-musicians – who stood by him loyally except when they found him difficult to get on with.

Schubert's life was not well organised, but he managed to subsist on casual earnings from teaching and the publication of a small proportion of his output, and on the generosity of those who believed in him. His life was dominated by the impulse to compose, and neither sickness nor any other misfortune did anything to weaken the driving force of his imagination. It may well be that his early death was partly due to the intensity with which he worked in his early years. Of his life's total of nearly 1,000 compositions roughly 600 were written before he was 21. An examination of his chamber music shows a similar proportion: only one-third was written in the last ten years of his life.

If we apply Mayrhofer's judgement to Schubert's music we shall find it difficult to speak of coarseness. But tenderness, sensuality and candour, sociability and melancholy are all there. It is traditional to emphasise the fact that of the composers commonly grouped together as 'the Viennese school' Schubert was the only one to be born in the city. In fact his origins were farther north: his father came from Moravia, his mother from Silesia, and there is in his music a toughness which has nothing to do with the traditional Viennese charm. He could succumb to that charm, as Brahms did later, but it was never a dominant influence in his work. What is charming in his music is much more the expression of his own personality – a sunny enjoyment of life which is often ready to turn to tears and which by its very happiness can bring tears to a listener's eyes. To him there were no hard and fast categories of music – serious and austere on the one hand, and light-hearted and gay on the other. In symphonies, sonatas and chamber music he could strike a note of desperate, even tragic, seriousness and then turn aside in another movement, or within the same movement, to a merry tune or a sentimental digression.

QUINTET IN A MAJOR FOR PIANO AND STRINGS (D. 667)

Throughout his life he was making music with others: with his family, with his fellow-choristers, with his friends and with professional musicians. It seems appropriate, therefore, to start a discussion of his chamber music with two works which illustrate his sociability better than others: the Quintet in A major for piano and strings, D. 667[1] (1819) and the Octet in F major for wind and strings, D. 803 (1824). Both these works were written for the conditions that he himself loved. Neither of them was intended in the first place for public performance: they were commissioned by amateurs who wanted something new to play. Sylvester Paumgartner, for whom the Quintet was written, was an amateur cellist with plenty of money, who lived at Steyr and organised music meetings in his house. Count Ferdinand von Troyer, who commissioned the Octet, was by all accounts an accomplished clarinettist, in whose lodgings in Vienna the work was first performed. The two works have nothing in common beyond the evident desire to give pleasure and the fact that each of them includes variations on one of Schubert's songs and a part for the double bass.

The double bass is not an entirely happy partner in the Quintet, where the other string instruments are violin, viola and cello.

[1] D. stands for Otto E. Deutsch, *Schubert: Thematic Catalogue of all his Works* (London, 1951).

A good deal of the writing is in the lower part of the instrument's compass, which results in a rather cavernous sound, particularly as the cello generally has an independent part. A typical example occurs in the early part of the development section of the first movement. This passage also illustrates one of the difficulties of combining the piano with strings. So long as the piano serves as an accompaniment there is no problem. But when string melodies, particularly sustained melodies, are transferred to the piano the discrepancy in tone can be disconcerting. The violin sonatas of Mozart and Beethoven are full of examples of the pretence that the piano is doing the same thing as the violin, whereas with its evanescent tone it is incapable of doing anything of the kind. In such cases the listener has to accept a suspension of disbelief, which is not impossible but is more difficult than it is in a work for piano solo. The relevant passage in Schubert's Quintet is from bars 147–70 of the first movement. The sustained melody for the violin is imitated by the piano, as a kind of substitute for flute and oboe, and developed further by the double bass:

EX. I

It is doubtful whether anyone who hears the work is seriously troubled by these problems of scoring. The music is so frank and open-hearted that it silences criticism of details. Schubert, on holiday in the summer of 1819, wrote to his brother Ferdinand: 'The country round Steyr is unimaginably lovely', and something of his delight in his surroundings flows over into this carefree music. It would not be inappropriate to describe the work as a *divertimento*. There are five movements:

8

The theme of the variations is borrowed from Schubert's song 'Die Forelle' (The Trout), D. 550 (1817), apparently at the suggestion of Paumgartner, who had a particular affection for it. This may very well have prompted him to write variations on songs in some of his later works – in the Octet (1824), the Introduction and Variations for flute and piano, D. 802 (1824), the String Quartet in D minor, D. 810 (1824), and the Fantasy in C major for violin and piano, D. 934 (1827). He also used material from his song 'Der Wanderer' ('Ich komme vom Gebirge her'), D. 493 (1816), in the Fantasy in C major for piano solo, D. 760 (1822).

Schubert's tonality was firmly based on the eighteenth-century tradition in which he grew up. But he loved to make excursions from the key, not merely in a development section (where it would be expected) but also in an exposition or even at the beginning of a movement. An exceptional instance is the first movement of the Piano Sonata in B major, D. 575 (1817), which deserts the tonic key after the first few bars and does not return to it until the end of the movement. The first movement of the Piano Quintet is less radical, but it does switch from A major to F major after the first ten bars, only to return to the principal key fifteen bars later. The return journey is simple but characteristic:

EX. 2

The added decoration in the third bar of this extract is also characteristic. Schubert did it again in the song 'An Silvia', D. 891 (1826):

EX. 3

dass ihr Al-les un - ter - than—
(That all are her vassals)

and in a rather different form in the first movement of the Piano Sonata in A major, D. 959 (1828), where a series of transformations lead to a fruitful development.

The opening of the first movement of the Quintet presents two elements which are strictly speaking unrelated but together play a vital part in what follows:

EX. 4

The arpeggio for the piano sounds like a simple preliminary flourish; but the triplets of which it is composed play a dominant role in the movement. Their bubbling rhythm is rarely absent and provides an effective foil to the second element, the sustained melody on the strings. The melody is not striking in itself: it has that neutral character which is very common in Schubert's large-scale instrumental works. But it contains within itself the seeds of development, and the dactylic rhythm in the fifth bar, equally characteristic, also proves to be influential. When Schubert eventually reaches E major by a slightly roundabout route he introduces a countermelody to his theme and then repeats the theme in the minor with significant alterations. The most dramatic example of key change occurs at the end of the exposition, where the expected conclusion in E major is temporarily interrupted by a switch to D major:

EX. 5

The same happy accident recurs, transposed, at the end of the movement. The development, beginning in C major (Ex. 1, p. 7), wanders happily through a variety of keys before it plunges into the recapitulation in D major.

The Andante begins with an attempt at tranquillity, but decoration starts breaking in almost immediately and runs through the greater part of the movement, roughly three-fifths of which are not in the key of F major. The Scherzo relies mainly on an impulsive rhythm and on effective contrasts between strings and piano. The theme of the Variations is presented in a simpler form than in the song, which, transposed into D major, begins:

EX. 6

(In a bright stream the capricious trout darted along like an arrow in joyous haste. I stood on the bank and, happily relaxed, watched the [lively little fish bathing in the clear water])

but the triplets of Schubert's original accompaniment provide a rhythmical background to three of the variations and eventually come into their own in the final Allegretto. In the first three variations the theme is heard successively in the treble, in an inner part and in the bass with little modification; but in the stormy Variation IV in D minor it is transformed. From D minor we move to B♭ major for Variation V; but B♭ major leads, by an irresistible Schubertian process, to D♭ major. The return from this key to D major for the final Allegretto is one of Schubert's happiest conjuring tricks. The structure of the last movement is simplicity itself. The second half is a carbon copy of the first but at a different pitch, to ensure that the work ends in A major. The rhythm of a military march, heard at the outset in the distance, drives the music inexorably to its conclusion, and the triplets which flourished in the first two movements are here again to add gaiety to the scene.

OCTET IN F MAJOR FOR WIND AND STRINGS (D. 803)

It has been supposed, though without positive evidence, that Count von Troyer commissioned the Octet as a companion piece to Beethoven's Septet in E♭ major, Op. 20 (1799), with which it is often paired in concerts today, though the Septet is a markedly inferior work. The resemblances in structure and in instrumentation are certainly striking. Both works have six movements, both include variations, both have a minuet as well as a scherzo, though they occur in a different order. The wind instruments are the same: clarinet, horn and bassoon. The only difference in scoring is that Schubert has added a second violin to Beethoven's violin, viola, cello and double bass. This gives him an ensemble comparable to a small orchestra, and in fact the string section is often treated in an orchestral way, with first and second violins in octaves and the double bass doubling the cello an octave below and so avoiding the clumsiness with which the instrument is treated in the Quintet.

The Octet is one of Schubert's longest instrumental works, but it never sounds tedious in performance, except possibly for the fourth movement, because the invention is consistently fertile and the scoring, particularly for the wind instruments, is full of variety. Count von Troyer would have had no cause to complain of the clarinet part, which offers every possible opportunity for expressive *cantabile* and brilliant execution; but this is true also of the bassoon and horn parts. A horn-player who can do justice to the coda of the first movement or of the minuet must be a master of his instrument. The six movements are as follows:

I Adagio – Allegro – Più allegro (F major)
II Adagio[1] (B♭ major)
III Scherzo: Allegro vivace (F major, with Trio in C major)
IV Theme and Variations: Andante – Un poco più mosso – Più lento (C major)
V Menuetto:[2] Allegretto (F major, with Trio in B♭ major)
VI Andante molto – Allegro – Andante molto[3] – Allegro molto (F major)

The first movement relies heavily on a dotted rhythm which is heard already in the slow introduction. Dotted rhythms also occur incidentally in the Adagio and very emphatically in the Scherzo. The slow introduction is another example of that inclination to abandon the key which has been mentioned already in connection with the Quintet. After a few bars in F major the music moves into A♭ major. Just when it appears to be moving back to F major it switches to D♭ major, and from there makes a subtle return to the tonic key, though uncertain whether to be major or minor until the last moment. Here is the first part of this transition:

EX. 7

[1] Andante un poco mosso in the first edition.
[2] The conventional spelling in Germany and Austria of the Italian *minuetto*.
[3] Misprinted Allegro molto in some miniature scores.

There are equally felicitous harmonic touches in the closely knit Allegro, which includes in its development a quotation from the introduction; but it is above all the buoyant rhythmical energy that impresses here.

In the Adagio, which in deference to Count von Troyer begins with a clarinet solo, the tranquillity which was missing in the slow movement of the Quintet is maintained: the music, lyrical in quality, is conceived in broad paragraphs. Curiously enough, the horn, which is so prominent in the first movement, has only a limited role here. It is silent for the first 40 bars and hardly emerges as a soloist until the latter part of the movement, and even then only intermittently. It is not, however, a negligible voice, and when it engages in dialogue with the clarinet and bassoon the effect is magical:

EX. 8

The Scherzo, one of the most exuberant of Schubert's movements in this form, has a suggestion of the open country – a hunting party, perhaps. On the other hand in the Andante we seem to be in a Viennese café or beer garden, listening to the homely strains of a local band. The theme is taken from a duet in Schubert's *Die Freunde von Salamanka* (The Friends from Salamanca), D. 326 (1815), an opera with dialogue written at the age of 18 but, like most of his stage music, never performed in his lifetime:

EX. 9

(Lying under the bright canopy of the trees, by the silver stream, the shepherd longs for his fair one and laments in rapturous song)

Though one can understand that Schubert had an affection for the pretty tune, it is difficult to see how he can have imagined that it was suitable material for variation. In fact the successive variations, though effectively scored, do little more than go through the motions, with concessions to virtuosity for the first violin: the only one that strikes a genuinely poetic note is No. 5 in C minor.

The Minuet is as popular in style as the Variations, but it is not naïve. It is also a genuine dance, not a conventional form, with the Trio strongly suggesting the rhythm of the *Ländler*. It is fascinating here, as so often in Schubert's work, to see how he will use harmonic adventures to twist mere tunefulness into an artistic experience. An example is the return to the opening theme in the main section of the Minuet:

EX. 10

The opening of the Finale strikes a note of solemnity for which nothing in the previous movements has prepared us. At the time when Schubert was writing the Octet, as well as the string quartets in A minor, D. 804, and D minor, D. 810, he was unwell and depressed, partly on account of his health and partly because he had written two operas which had not been accepted for performance. It is possible to see a reflection of his state of mind in both the quartets, and it would be tempting to attribute the sombre opening of the Finale of the Octet to the same cause. But the relation between a man's music and his life is never as simple as this. Creative artists have the unique power of dissociating themselves from their bodily ills and mental distress. It is well known that some of Sullivan's gayest music was written when he was suffering acute pain. The prevailing mood of Schubert's Octet is so sunny that it is probably a mistake to regard the opening of the Finale as a relapse into a confession of unhappiness. This music is not tortured in expression or even sad: it is sombre, like some of Haydn's introductions, in order that what follows will make a stronger impression by contrast. Its recurrence in the course of the movement can then be interpreted not as a reminder of grief but as a powerful dramatic stroke.

Schubert, more than any other composer, seems to have discovered the secret of perpetual motion or at least to have found a way of suggesting that the music is never likely to stop. Familiar examples are the finale of the C major Symphony, D. 944, and the last movement of the Piano Sonata in C minor, D. 958. In the Finale of the Octet the themes are simple but they seem to contain within themselves the seeds of endless development; and all the time there is a pulsing rhythm which stops only to allow the music to get its second wind. Just when we seem to be nearing what the programme analysts call a 'brilliant conclusion' the music of the introduction returns, and there is still enough energy left for a headlong coda.

STRING QUINTET IN C MAJOR (D. 956)

The bulk of Schubert's chamber music consists of quartets, trios and sonatas. Apart from three very early works – an Overture in C minor for string quintet, D. 8 (1811), an Octet in F major for wind instruments, D. 72 (1813), and *Eine kleine Trauermusik* in Eb minor for nine wind instruments, D. 79 (1813) – the only exceptions are the Piano Quintet and the Octet which have just been discussed and the String Quintet in C major, D. 956 (1828).

The String Quintet was written during the last months of Schubert's life – a time that saw also the composition of the songs published as *Schwanengesang,* D. 957, and the last three piano sonatas, D. 958—60. Unlike Mozart, whose quintets included two violas, Schubert followed Boccherini in writing for two cellos. Maurice Brown[1] suggests that 'to Schubert (who himself played the viola), it was, in general, a filling-in instrument' and that in the Quintet 'the viola is, if not negligible, subordinate'. A study of the score of the Quintet hardly supports this view, and few viola-players would agree with it. It is true that, except in the Trio of the Scherzo, the viola does not emerge as a solo instrument, but the same is true of the other members of the ensemble. In all four movements the viola plays its part in dealing with the melodic material, and no one who has heard the work will forget the duet between viola and cello in the recapitulation of the first movement. By using two cellos Schubert is able to reinforce the bass by making them play occasionally in unison or in octaves; but he also has the opportunity of using the first cello as a melodic instrument in the upper part of its compass, either alone or doubling the first violin in the lower octave: there is a long, ecstatic section of the slow movement where the two instruments continue in this way for nearly 30 bars of slow time.

Schubert has the habit of beginning a first movement with a statement which is remarkable not for its melodic interest but for the expectancy which it creates. The opening of the 'Unfinished' Symphony, D. 759 (1822), is a familiar example; others will be found in the piano sonatas. The *cantabile* melody which opens the A minor Quartet, D. 804, is an exception to his general practice. In the first movement of the String Quintet what we first hear is a harmonic progression, which may have suggested to Brahms the opening of his third symphony, and this dissolves into music which is inconclusive because it leads one to expect that something more significant will follow. What follows immediately is a complementary statement played by the second violin, viola and the two cellos – a dark sonority which provides a perfect contrast to the brightness of the opening. A string quintet is parti-

[1] *Schubert: a Critical Biography* (London, 1958), p. 226.

cularly suitable for such contrasts, as Mozart was well aware; but apart from the opening of the movement and the recapitulation Schubert ignores this possibility and takes advantage rather of the richness of texture that five instruments can provide and the opportunity of doubling melodic lines.

A stormy version of the opening material, with the melody ground out by the two cellos, leads to a conventional cadence, from which emerges, with a kind of voluptuous reluctance, a duet which offers relaxations:

EX. 11

The new key of E♭ major, however, is not established; the music reverts almost nostalgically to C major and from there proceeds to a cadence in G major which allows the whole process to be repeated, with the duet this time given to the violins. This leads once again to G major, in which key the exposition ends with an abrupt, march-like passage preceding a lingering reminiscence of Ex. 11 (the two cellos are in unison):

EX. 12

An epigrammatic postscript of this kind is very much in Haydn's manner: and like Haydn, Schubert selects it for development, brushing aside the reminiscence of Ex. 11. The treatment is ruthless, involving wholesale repetition in a different key, and might even seem mechanical, if it were not for the wonderful sense of release that occurs when the music returns to the opening statement of the movement, accompanied by a kind of ghostly echo of the marching rhythm of the development.

Few composers knew better than Schubert how to move in a slow tempo. The Adagio of the Quintet moves so deliberately that motion itself seems suspended. The brief interjections of the first violin do nothing to disturb the effortless progress of a melody which pursues its tranquil course for the space of 28 bars. The tranquillity is rudely broken by a change of key (E major to F minor) and a turbulent accompaniment above which the first violin and first cello pour out the passionate strain to which reference has already been made. When the opening section returns there is considerable embellishment from the first violin and the second cello, but it is little more than a ripple on the surface.

The Scherzo, which is developed at considerable length, is a complete contrast: robust and uninhibited, with suggestions from time to time of hunting horns. The most striking feature of this movement, however, is the Trio. Other composers have written trios in a slower tempo, and Beethoven in the 'Pastoral' Symphony wrote one in a different rhythm. But Schubert's idea of introducing a slow Trio in 4/4 time was completely original. The significance of the change is not immediately apparent. There is something enigmatic about this music, like a man mulling a problem over in his mind and starting again whenever he seems to have solved it. In an opera the meaning would be clear enough: here the very simplicity of the music is puzzling.

The last movement (Allegretto, not Allegro) is partly in the Hungarian idiom to which Schubert, like other Austrian composers, was addicted from time to time. Though it includes at least one melody of great charm, in a characteristic rhythm:

EX. 13

it is not equal in invention to the other movements. It seems at times to be moving for the sake of moving, as though the composer was in a hurry to finish the work and was not prepared to be too self-critical. Perhaps this is the explanation. Schubert wanted to get the Quintet published, as well as the three piano sonatas. A composer who could complete four works of this size in a comparatively short space of time could hardly afford to wait for ideas if they were not immediately forthcoming.

STRING QUARTETS

Schubert wrote more than 20 works for string quartet. Four of these have disappeared, and another five are either fragmentary or exist in an incomplete state. Of the remainder ten had been written before 1817, when Schubert was 20. The three quartets by which he is best known date from the years 1824–6. The earliest quartet to survive complete appears to be one in five movements, four of which are in different keys, D. 18 (1811–12). The first movement (Andante) is actually in no specific key at all. It begins in C minor, continues in D minor and ends in G minor with a cadence on the dominant chord in preparation for the next movement. The second movement (Presto) begins and ends in G minor, but much of it is in D major and D minor. The third movement (Minuet) is in F major, with a Trio in C major. The fourth movement (Andante) is in B♭ major, with sections in F major. The fifth movement (Presto) has its first section in B♭ major, but abandons this in favour of C major, returning to the original key almost at the last moment. It would be a mistake to attribute this unusual key structure to Schubert's inexperience. Even at this age he must have been sufficiently familiar with quartets by Haydn and Mozart to know that this was not a normal procedure. The most likely explanation is that he was experimenting. The experiment was awkward and unconvincing, but it may well have been the first sign of an adventurous attitude to tonality which stayed with him all his life. The significant signs of immaturity in this quartet are the inability to continue or develop the ideas and the attempt at contrapuntal writing without any capacity for it.

The same signs appear in the D major Quartet, D. 94, which is dated 'not later than 1814' in the *Gesamtausgabe* but is certainly earlier and probably contemporary with the Quartet 'in mixed keys', D. 18. The first movement is full of ideas, any one of which would prove fruitful in the hands of an experienced composer. But the young Schubert does not know what to do with them: he throws away his opportunities. The music keeps stopping and starting again. Towards the end of the exposition it moves into A major but comes back again to the tonic key; the situation is saved at the last moment by a hasty cadence in A major. The development section wanders all over the place without saying anything convincing. It was natural for Schubert to be influenced by the music that he heard and played. The slow movement of this quartet begins like an echo of Haydn; the Minuet reproduces exactly the rhythm of the Scherzo of Beethoven's second symphony. Naïve as this music is, there is nothing in it that would have justified an impartial observer in saying that the composer had no talent. The natural gift was there: all that was needed was discipline. Discipline is something that can be encouraged by a teacher; but in the long run a composer has to learn to discipline himself. In a sense that was something that Schubert was learning all his life.

By October 1812 he had already acquired a firmer grasp of his material. This is evident from the Quartet in C major, D. 32.[1] There is still a tendency for the longer movements to sprawl; but the Minuet is neatly organised, and the Finale compensates for a lack of cohesion by a convincing display of energy. The opening of this movement deserves to be quoted here:

EX. 14

Allegro con spirito

In November of the same year Schubert embarked on another quartet, this time in B♭ major, D. 36, but did not finish it until

[1] The *Gesamtausgabe* printed only the first movement (Presto) and the Minuet, adding the second half of the Finale in the *Revisionsbericht*. The complete work in four movements, edited by Maurice Brown, was published for the first time in 1956 by Breitkopf & Härtel, Wiesbaden.

February 1813. The first movement experiments with contra-puntal devices which must be described as courageous rather than inevitable, but on the whole the structure is tauter and there is less evidence of marking time. If the style of writing often seems orchestral, that is understandable in view of Schubert's experience at the Konvikt,[1] where orchestral playing was part of the educa-tion of the choristers. There is nothing discursive about the Andante or the Minuet, and the Finale (a rondo) makes a brave attempt at perpetual motion in Haydn's manner though without Haydn's avoidance of unessentials. No one would have described the boy as a prodigy. What is important is that he was learning in the best possible way – by making mistakes. The mastery of his last three quartets (1824–6) is the result of the persistence shown in hammering out his technique in these early years.

Four quartets survive from the year 1813: C major, D. 46, B♭ major, D. 68 (of which only two movements are extant), D major, D. 74, and E♭ major, D. 87. The C major Quartet, written appar-ently in five days, shows a remarkable advance on its predecessors. The counterpoint is assured and is used not as a self-conscious device but as an integral part of the music. It is beautifully handled in the Adagio which introduces the first movement:

EX. 15

[1] The Imperial Seminary, which included the choristers of the Court Chapel among its pupils.

24

The chromatic figure turns up again in the Allegro con moto that follows and helps to bind the whole movement together. The Finale has a buoyancy and a sense of direction that one misses in the earlier quartets: there is no uncertainty here and no waste matter. The only passage that raises some doubts is the Trio of the Minuet, which switches rather too abruptly from Bb major to C major. The two surviving movements of the Bb major Quartet are of a quality that makes one regret the loss of the slow movement and the Minuet. The exuberance of the first movement culminates in a dramatic use of the Neapolitan sixth in the closing bars, and there is an equally dramatic moment at the end of the Finale (a movement which happily imitates Haydn's methods of surprise), where the music diverges into Gb major before it makes a triumphant cadence in the tonic key.

The first movement of the D major Quartet, on the other hand, has little to offer beyond amiability, and the ending is too obvious a reminiscence of the overture of Mozart's *Die Zauberflöte*:

EX. 16

Mozart's influence seems to hover also over the Finale, which begins as if it were entitled 'On hearing the Paris Symphony'. On the whole this is a disappointing work. The slow movement is insipid. Only the Minuet – a form in which Schubert was always happy – matches technique with invention. The Eb major Quartet is in a very different category. By the time he started work on it in November Schubert had left the Konvikt, had written his first symphony and begun to write his first opera, *Des Teufels Lust-schloss* (The Devil's Castle), D. 84. He was now sure of himself. No doubt there is a good deal that is derivative in this quartet. Schubert learned much from his predecessors; but the most important lesson he learned was how to put a movement together. He also learned the value of an open texture, and how to be effective without trying to be clever. All the string quartets are well written for the instruments, but this is the first one that sounds like chamber music from start to finish; and it has a splendidly impetuous Scherzo.

The E♭ major Quartet was published two years after Schubert's death as No. 1 of Op. 125; No. 2 was the E major Quartet, D. 35♭ (1816). The only complete works between these two are the B♭ major Quartet, D. 112 (1814), published in 1863 as Op. 168, and the G minor Quartet, D. 173 (1815). These are both works of considerable charm but not of outstanding originality, with the exception of the Finale of the first. The key of G minor was almost bound to bring back memories of Mozart, which occur in the recapitulation of the first movement (a treatment of the principal theme which does not appear in the exposition):

EX. 17

This movement is unusual in that the recapitulation begins unmistakably in B♭ major and then moves to G minor – the reverse of what happens in the exposition. A further peculiarity is that the end of the exposition is in D minor: this is adjusted in the end of the recapitulation so that the movement ends in the tonic key. All his life Schubert was fascinated by key relationships and frequently worked out new sequences. The slow movement of the B♭ major Quartet begins in G minor and has a second section in F major. This leads straight into a recapitulation which begins in D minor and moves first to E♭ major and then to B♭ major. Since F major led to D minor, B♭ major will lead to G minor, in which key we hear the opening strain again. It is a very simple scheme, but very effective, all the more because, after the relatively quiet music that has gone before, there is a sudden outburst just before the end for all four instruments on Ab: it occurs twice and is followed by a cadence which dissolves into the softest *pianissimo*.

Schubert was in the habit of dating his early quartets. In the case of the Bb major Quartet he dated all four movements, and for good measure noted at the end of the first movement: 'In $4\frac{1}{2}$ Stunden verfertigt' (completed in $4\frac{1}{2}$ hours) – which does not mean that there were no ideas in his head or rough drafts on paper before he began. The Finale of this quartet is unlike any other composer's work and unlike anything that Schubert himself had written earlier. It begins with a smooth, steady movement for the lower strings, against which the first violin has an intermittent dancing pattern:

EX. 18

Before long the dancing pattern becomes insistent and eventually spreads to the other parts. We begin to suspect that we are hearing a ghostly premonition of the Scherzo of the C major Symphony, D. 944, and the suspicion becomes stronger when we reach this passage:

EX. 19

The E major Quartet shows Schubert experimenting still further with the possibilities of key-contrast. In the first movement he also forecasts his later practice of abandoning the principal key at quite an early stage: the second section of the exposition, basically in B major, is much longer than the first. (Schubert's love for Mozart is apparent again in the opening melody of the B major section.) He was rarely content to recapitulate a movement exactly. Either the material is in a different order, or something is omitted or added, or the sequence of keys is extended. In this first movement the recapitulation begins normally in E major: but the section corresponding to the B major section of the exposition is in G major and only later comes round to the principal key of the movement. There are also experiments in the Andante; but this is on the whole a colourless movement. To write a convincing slow movement demanded a maturity of thought which was still outside Schubert's grasp. The Finale, however, is triumphantly successful. It might be said to acknowledge the existence of Haydn's 'Gipsy' Rondo and the finale of Mozart's Eb major symphony, K. 543, but it goes its own independent way with a bubbling assurance which is captivating: only sour critics would say that it overstays its welcome.

By the end of 1816, the year of the E major Quartet, Schubert had already written five symphonies and five operas. Between that date and 1824, when the A minor Quartet, D. 804, was written, he composed two more symphonies and five more operas, as well as several piano sonatas and a host of other works. The only complete chamber works written during this period were a Sonata in A major for violin and piano, D. 574, a String Trio in Bb major, D. 581, and the Piano Quintet. There are two possible reasons for this lull in production: one, that he was too busy with other things; the other, that he was dissatisfied with what he had already done and wanted to wait until he was certain that he could do himself justice. The second reason is not implausible. It is significant that he began a Quartet in C minor, D. 703, in 1820 but failed to finish it. All that exists is the first movement (Allegro assai)[1] and part of an Andante in Ab major. Schubert, like Mozart, left quite a number of unfinished works. The explanation must be that if a piece did not seem to be going right there was no point in tinkering with it: it was better to put it on one side and start

---

[1] The Germans call this *Quartettsatz*, which simply means 'quartet movement'. There seems to be no justification for using this as a title in other countries.

on something else. In the case of this quartet one must suppose that Schubert felt dissatisfied with the Andante. He certainly had no cause for dissatisfaction with the first movement, which is perfectly constructed and passionate in expression. There is more here than assurance and economy of material, though both of these are striking. What the movement reveals is the insight that only the most gifted composers have possessed, the capacity for seeing that one thing must follow another, that development lies in the material and needs only to be released, that notes, as Mendelssohn pointed out, can say more than words.

A formal analysis of the movement might lead to the conclusion that the structure is unusual: but this would have to be qualified by the realisation that form is different in all Schubert's mature works – there is no standard procedure. Here, in the simplest possible terms, is the plan of this movement:

Exposition: A: C minor
                  B: (a) Ab major
                     (b) Ab minor, modulating through C minor to
                     (c) G major
Development: Based largely on the rhythm of A
Recapitulation: B: (a) Bb major and Eb major
                     (b) Eb minor, modulating to
                     (c) C major
                  A: C minor

It gives no indication of the ingenuity with which the opening phrase:

EX. 20

is woven into the fabric of the whole movement, not necessarily in literal terms but in the shape of an insistent rhythm. The phrase itself has a dramatic intensity which is new in Schubert's chamber music, an intensity which is all the more powerful because it begins quietly. It is impossible to quote all the variants which arise out of this phrase. One of them occurs as early as bar 13:

EX. 21

and this is clearly the spiritual father of that nostalgic passage towards the end of the exposition which, more than anything else in this movement, lingers obstinately in the ear once it has been heard:

EX. 22

Throughout the movement the string writing has a clarity which is an object-lesson to anyone who aspires to write a string quartet. No later developments in string-writing can do anything to weaken our admiration for the mastery that Schubert shows here. That he failed to complete the work is something that it is difficult not to deplore.

The Allegro assai of the C minor Quartet dates from December 1820. Just over three years later Schubert turned again to the composition of quartets. There seems no doubt that this was at least partly due to his acquaintance with Ignaz Schuppanzigh, who was not only a distinguished violinist but also the leader of a celebrated quartet. The first work to spring from this new impulse was the A minor Quartet, D. 804, which was probably written in January or early February 1824. According to Schubert's young friend, the painter Moritz von Schwind, Schuppanzigh was 'quite enthusiastic' about the new work. His quartet performed it publicly on 15 March, 'rather slowly in Schubert's opinion', according to Schwind. The press reports were non-committal, but the audience appears to have appreciated the work, which was published in September under the title 'Trois Quattours [*sic*] ... Œuv. 29: no. 1.' The second quartet of the three implied by the title was presumably the D minor, D. 810, the first movement of which was certainly written in March of this year though the work was not performed till 1826. It was first published, without an opus number, three years after Schubert's death. The G major Quartet, D. 887, composed in 1826, had to wait even longer for a publisher. In fact, apart from the *Rondeau brillant* for violin and piano, D. 895 (1826), the A minor Quartet was the only piece of chamber music by Schubert to be published in his lifetime.[1] The frustrating experience of failing to find the outlet and the money that he needed may well have delayed the composition of the G major Quartet, since he wrote in a letter dated 31 March 1824 that he had composed two quartets and wanted to write a third.

The letter, addressed to Leopold Kupelwieser, begins with a pathetic confession of despair and misery. One of the reasons for this was ill-health. It would seem that Schubert had not completely recovered from the effects of the venereal disease which he had contracted in 1822 and which had necessitated a period in hospital in 1823. But there seems to be more in what he says than a lament for ill-health. There is an impression that the composer has lost faith in himself – an experience familiar to every creative artist. That this experience did not necessarily affect the music he wrote is clear, as we have seen, from the Octet, which dates from the same period. But it does seem to have left its mark on the A minor Quartet and perhaps on the D minor Quartet as well. In this letter Schubert quotes the words of Gretchen at the spinning-wheel which he had set so perfectly as a boy:

> Meine Ruh' ist hin, mein Herz ist schwer,
> Ich finde sie nimmer und nimmer mehr.
>
> (My peace is gone, my heart is heavy,
> I can never find it again)

Something of the mood of the song has filtered into the first movement of the A minor Quartet, particularly in the restless accompaniment which starts two bars before a melody is heard.

[1] According to the publisher, Probst of Leipzig, the E♭ major Piano Trio, D. 929, was engraved before Schubert died, but it is not known whether it was actually published before it was announced for sale in December 1828. See p. 47.

There is an even more direct relation with a song in the opening
of the Minuet:

EX. 23

These desolate strains are unmistakably a reminiscence, if not an
actual borrowing, from the song known as 'Die Gotter Griechen-
lands' (The gods of Greece), D. 677 (1819), the title of Schiller's
poem from which the text is taken. The song begins:

EX. 24

(Fair world, where art thou?)

But the quartet as a whole does not express suffering or regret.
The slow movement breathes happiness, even though it is the
happiness that can bring tears, and the Finale has something of the
atmosphere of rural jollity.

The introductory bars of the first movement are not a complete
innovation. Mozart had done this in his G minor symphony.
K. 550, and again in his last piano concerto in B♭ major, K. 595,
but these are both exceptional instances. The procedure is also
exceptional in Schubert: the nearest parallel is the first movement
of the 'Unfinished' Symphony, where the tremulous semiquavers
recall the song 'Suleika I' ('Was bedeutet die Bewegung'), D. 720
(1821), in the same key; but there the accompaniment figure does

not begin the movement. It is remarkable that Schubert, who wrote so many songs, almost invariably avoids beginning an instrumental movement with anything that sounds like the opening of a song. To him the two categories were normally distinct. In the A minor Quarter it is not only the restless stirring of the lower strings that suggests a song; the melody introduced by the first violin in the third bar is very much a song tune and for some time remains within a singer's normal range. Here are its first eight bars:

EX. 25

After a varied repetition it appears in the major key. Schubert was always inclined to regard major and minor as two sides of the same coin: one can never foresee when he is going to switch from one to the other and back again, and often it happens, as in the song 'Der Wegweiser' (The sign-post) from *Die Winterreise* (The Winter Journey), D. 911 (1827), and also here, that the major is more pathetic in effect than the minor. The tranquillity is soon shattered by a brief but stormy development of the figure marked *a* in Ex. 25. There is no transition to the second principal theme: the music comes to a halt, exactly as it might in a song, and is followed by another song-like melody in C major, which in its turn is treated to development. Development of material within an exposition is characteristic of Schubert's later works and may result in surprises, such as the brief passage in A♭ major before the final cadence in C major.

The development section proper, which is relatively short, is devoted entirely to the opening theme and particularly to the figure marked *b* in Ex. 25. This is a highly imaginative treatment, since the figure has no independent melodic significance but is carved out of the complete melody and given a new life of its own, including imitation and contrapuntal accompaniment. But it is figure *a* that leads us very deliberately to the recapitulation. Here the second theme appears in A major, but at the end the major key is rudely brushed aside and we have a coda in A minor which

C   33

muses on the opening theme. In the violent cadence *a* is heard for the last time on viola and cello.

At the end of 1823 Schubert had lavished some delightful incidental music, D. 797, on a preposterous play, *Rosamunde, Fürstin von Cypern* (Rosamund, Princess of Cyprus). The play had only two performances, though the music was well received, particularly the overture.[1] The vocal pieces were published, with piano accompaniment, in March 1824, but the Entr'acte in B♭ major after Act III, which has for many years been one of Schubert's most popular pieces, was still in manuscript.[2] The composer's affection for it is evident from the fact that he transposed the main section into C major and used it, with minor alterations, as the principal theme of the slow movement of the A minor Quartet. It is difficult to see why he did not write a series of variations on it, as he did with the very similar theme of the Impromptu in B♭ major, D. 935, no. 3 (1827) for piano. Instead he wrote an extended movement which sounds at first as if it were going to be a rondo but in which the borrowed theme appears only twice. Tacked on to it is a second section which, beginning in C major, settles down into G major, with a characteristic side-glance at G minor. After the main theme has been heard for the second time there is a development which imposes on the pretty tune a strain which it is hardly able to bear. The rest of the movement is a recapitulation in C major of the material previously heard in the dominant key. This is perhaps the place to mention that the rhythm ♩ ♫ which recurs in the *Rosamunde* tune used in the quartet is a favourite one with Schubert. It is found, for instance, in the Impromptu just mentioned and occurs as early as the 10 Variations on an original theme for piano, D. 156 (1815). However, it is not peculiar to Schubert. A familiar example is the Allegretto of Beethoven's seventh symphony, Op. 92 (1812), which may conceivably have influenced him: but it occurs also in a string

---

[1] The overture was one that Schubert had originally sketched for his opera *Alfonso und Estrella*, D. 732 (1822–3), which he failed to get performed. What is generally known as the *Rosamunde* Overture was a completely rewritten version of his Overture in D major, D. 590 (1817), used as an overture to the play *Die Zauberharfe* (The Magic Harp), D. 644 (1820).

[2] It was eventually published in 1866.

quartet in E major, Op. 3, by Anselm Hüttenbrenner, from which Schubert borrowed a theme for variations, D. 576 (1817), and there may very well be examples in the works of other composers of the time – which does not alter the fact that it became one of Schubert's finger-prints.

The relationship of the Minuet to the song 'Die Götter Grie-chenlands' has already been mentioned. It is unique among Schubert's minuets and scherzos, not only in the modal flavour of the opening figure (Ex. 23, p. 32) but also in its suggestion of a world where comfort cannot be expected – the world of a child who is bewildered by suffering. The wonderful modulation to Ab major in the second section does nothing to weaken this impression; nor does the Trio, in A major, which seems to offer not consolation but rather a mere distraction from grief. It is superficially a simple movement: but in its very simplicity lies the secret of its appeal.

The Finale is consistently cheerful. It is rather like one of those peasant dances that one finds in the operas of Weber and Marschner – a townsman's view of the way in which country folk enjoy themselves. The dance rhythm is so persistent that one almost expects to hear a tambourine in the background. One day an astute choreographer will realise its possibilities for ballet, if this has not happened already. The structure of the movement, a rondo, is ingenious. The principal section in A major does not recur complete. It is divided into two parts, the first of which recurs before the development and the second after it. As so often with Schubert the exposition is in more than two principal keys. It begins in A major, with side-glances at A minor and E major, proceeds to C♯ minor (on a jiggy rhythm) and ends in E major. The recapitulation, after a dramatic hiatus at the end of the development, begins with the side-glances, this time in F♯ minor and A major, settles down in A major, proceeds by analogy to F♯ minor (the jiggy rhythm) and ends in A major. It is a light-weight movement, which makes no attempt to strike attitudes, except at the end of the development and at the final cadence, where the two decisive *ff* chords occur just at the point where the *decrescendo* seems to be nearing vanishing point.

The D minor Quartet is anything but a light-weight work. The mood on the whole is sombre, even tragic. It is often abrupt in expression and makes defiant gestures. There are moments when the tension is relaxed, but there is nothing to correspond to the unaffected charm that provides a contrast in its predecessor. The first movement has a kind of ruthless logic that has no exact parallel in Schubert's work, though many of its procedures are similar to those in other works of his maturity. We begin with a challenge, which is almost immediately hushed, as if it were suddenly conscious of its over-boldness:

EX. 26

The music then starts marching forwards, with the triplet rhythm supplying the motive power:

EX. 27

until eventually there is a restatement of the opening, which explodes into a violent surge of triplets:

EX. 28

The mood softens as we reach the key of F major, but the triplet rhythm still continues:

EX. 29

There is a brief break in the tension before the presentation of a tune with a strongly Italian flavour:

EX. 30

Schubert's admiration for Rossini appears in other instrumental works, notably the two overtures, in D major and C major, D. 590 and 591 (both 1817), and the sixth symphony, D. 589 (1818), not to mention the 'great' C major Symphony, D. 944 (1828). Ex. 30 is the kind of melody that does not immediately suggest development; but Schubert takes it in hand and subjects it to vigorous contrapuntal treatment, ending with a cadence in A minor, which, with A major as an alternative, is the principal key of the rest of the exposition.

Here is the opening of the contrapuntal development of Ex. 30:

EX. 31

The little figure marked *x* is extracted and given to the second violin and viola in the cadential bar. It gradually assumes increasing importance until the music softens into A major, when it serves as a counterpoint to a restatement of Ex. 30. The triplet rhythm had disappeared during the contrapuntal development, but it now reappears on the viola, using the version previously heard in Ex. 29. In this way three quite distinct elements which had previously been heard separately are brought together and combined:

EX. 32

As the music increases in intensity the cello abruptly calls for silence with an abbreviated version of the figure *x*. The melody of Ex. 30 begins to die away through a melting modulation but eventually reasserts itself in A minor, in spite of renewed protests from the cello, and so brings the exposition to an end. The form of the exposition may be roughly summarised as follows:

A: 1 – D minor (Ex. 26)
    2 – D minor (Ex. 27)
    3 – D minor (Ex. 28), modulating to
B: 1 – F major (Ex. 29)
    2 – F major (Ex. 30), developed (Ex. 31) and modulating to
    3 – A minor
    4 – A major (Ex. 32)
    5 – A minor

The tautness of this construction disproves the generalisation that Schubert's expositions are diffuse. That he is sometimes tempted to wander is undeniable; but here there is nothing irrelevant.

How is this complex material to be developed? The second violin suggests an answer by beginning with the figure *x*, but this is dismissed by a recollection of Ex. 30 and though it is heard briefly fluttering on the first violin it plays no further part in the development, which is concise: it is based mainly on Ex. 30, under which is heard at one point a restatement of A2 (Ex. 27) in F♯ minor. Ex. 30 eventually becomes nothing more than an accompaniment to sinister mutterings in the rhythm of A1 (Ex. 26) which lead to the recapitulation. The recapitulation takes the following form:

A: 3 – D minor, leading to
B: 1 – D major
   2 – D major, developed in D minor
   3 – D minor, modulating to
   4 – B♭ major
   5 – D minor

The coda follows, based on A2 and subsiding to a *pianissimo* ending by way of one of Schubert's most fascinating modulations, which is repeated. Here is the end of the movement, beginning with the repetition of the modulation:[1]

EX. 33

Throughout the movement one has the impression of an imagination working at high pressure and an intelligence which is firmly in control.

The slow movement consists of variations on material taken from Schubert's early song 'Der Tod und das Mädchen' (Death

---

[1] Strictly speaking this is not a modulation, since the music remains in the key of D minor. But the listener hears it as a modulation to E♭ minor, only to be checked by the discovery that the dominant seventh in that key has turned itself into an augmented sixth, so that we are back where we started.

and the girl),[1] D. 531 (1817), which has given its name to the whole quartet. It is not one of Schubert's most successful songs, since it adopts for the girl's protests an operatic manner which is unsuited to such a short poem. The text, by Matthias Claudius (1740–1815), is a dialogue between the two participants. Death appears as a skeleton to the girl, who shrinks in horror and cries 'Avaunt'. But Death reassures her: 'Bin Freund und komme nicht zu strafen' (I am a friend and do not come to punish you). She has nothing to fear: she will sleep safe in his arms. There is nothing morbid about the poem, though it does imply that death will be a welcome release. Whether this was in Schubert's mind when he was writing the quartet it is impossible to say. In the song he represents the approach of Death, before the girl begins to sing, by a solemn eight-bar introduction for the piano which, transposed and slightly modified, supplies the first section of the theme in the quartet. The first six bars of the second section of the theme are new: the remainder is taken from the accompaniment to Death's reply to the girl.

The theme, though rhythmically monotonous, is so simple that it is ideal material for variation, consisting as it does largely of harmonic progressions. The six variations do not entirely exclude decoration for the first violin, but there is none of the conventional tinsel which makes such a lavish display in the Piano Quintet and the Octet. The scheme of the variations is as follows:

I *pp*, with dynamic changes in the second section; theme in repeated triplets on second violin, with viola as a second part; counterpoint for first violin; cello *pizzicato*.

II *p*, with slight dynamic changes; variation of theme (derived from harmony) on cello; animated accompaniment for other strings.

III beginning *ff*, with some passages *pp*; vigorously rhythmical variation for all four strings, with broken texture in the second section.

IV *pp*, major key; suave *legato* writing for lower strings; decoration for first violin.

V first section *pp*, with *crescendo* to *ff* for the repeat; theme on viola, with second violin as second part; agitated accompaniment for first violin and cello: second section, agitation, *ff*, spreads to all the upper strings.

VI *pp*, diminishing to *ppp*: melodic variation in triplets for first violin, with simple accompaniment, gradually subsiding into the tranquil rhythm of the theme.

A short coda follows.

[1] Traditionally known in England as 'Death and the maiden', though there seems no reason for using an old-fashioned term for a perfectly ordinary German word.

The prevailing minor key, except in Variation IV, and the generally low level of dynamics combine to produce a sombre mood which is akin to that of the first movement. There is possibly some lack of variety, since the basic rhythm of the theme remains largely unchanged in all but one of the variations: but there is also a notable simplicity of treatment and a restraint that shows the hand of the mature artist.

The most striking feature of the Scherzo, which is marked 'Allegro molto', is the fierce syncopation which occurs in the opening bars:

EX. 34

and comes to dominate the main section. There is a Slavonic flavour here, which inevitably makes one think of Dvořák. The music sweeps forward with a great deal of emphasis both on and off the beat. The Trio, a tranquil and gracious section, is in D major but cannot resist relapsing into D minor on occasion. This is a movement that makes no pretence at subtlety: it makes its effect by the way in which it carries the listener irresistibly forward.

The Finale is a rondo in tarantella rhythm – a rhythm which Schubert used again in the G major Quartet and the C minor Piano Sonata. In both quartets there is a temporary break in the headlong pursuit of speed. In the D minor Quartet the break is made more dramatic by the fact that it is preceded by a pause. as though the dancers were for the moment out of breath. Not surprisingly, the change occurs at the point where the music has settled into the key of F major. In this key we hear a broad chorale-like phrase which seems to express a mood of unchallenge-able confidence. But the dance rhythm reasserts itself almost at once and impudently insists on appearing as a counterpoint to a repetition of the chorale. This interplay of two contrasted ideas continues for some time until breathless fragments of the taran-tella theme indicate that it is about to make its reappearance;

but in order to heighten the expectancy the reappearance is delayed until the last possible moment. The actual development is short. The recapitulation begins with the chorale-like theme, this time in B♭ major. The rest of the movement corresponds in essentials to the exposition, apart from the coda, which is marked Prestissimo. The impetuous character of this movement has sometimes led to the suggestion that it expresses a demoniac urge; but that is a mistaken interpretation. It is first and foremost a dance, which hardly ever slackens. Since much of it is quiet, it might be regarded as a ghostly dance, but this would be an unwise exercise of imagination. It is much more in the style of a folk dance which, because of its intensity, compels the dancers to be serious. If the coda suggests triumph, it is not the triumph of some imaginary demon but the intoxication of the dancers themselves, who, so to speak, cry 'Olé' before they fall breathless to the ground. One can imagine that even those who knew Schubert well were surprised by this extraordinary display of energy from the little man whom they knew as *Schwammerl* (Tubby).

The D minor Quartet, one of the finest works in the classical repertory, impresses by its unity of purpose. The G major Quartet, the last that Schubert wrote, is less single-minded and more ambitious, and its lyrical passages seem less in harmony with their context – which is not to deny the wealth of imagination to be found in it.[1] Nowhere is Schubert's equation of major and minor more striking than in the opening of the first movement – a neutral opening, but one charged with great possibilities:

EX. 35

[1] This work was presumably the 'new quartet' of which the first movement was performed at the concert of his music which Schubert gave in March 1828.

It is like an extravagant character is a play thrusting his head through the curtains before the action begins. The action here begins gradually, and the opening chords are seen to be part of it. But this section of the long exposition is relatively short. A chord of F♯ major leads gently into a curiously hesitant theme with a restricted range, the rhythm of which derives from three bars in the first section. The theme is in D major, and Schubert obviously likes it so much that he repeats it in the same key with trimmings for the first violin – a whispered vibration in triplets. The triplets play an important part in what follows, which is a development similar to the one in the first movement of the D minor Quartet. The development, so far from leading any-where, brings us back to a third statement of the 'hesitant theme', this time in B♭ major, with the cello as soloist and *pizzicato* accompaniment for the other strings. A similar development follows but once again leads to a restatement of the theme – its fourth appearance – this time in its original key. The viola plays the tune and the violin resumes its triplets, which take command when the theme is finished and drop down gradually to a subdued muttering on the cello:

EX. 36

This leads back to a repetition of the exposition. The second time it stirs up mutterings from the other strings and comes to play an important part in the development section, which is very much shorter than the exposition and includes material from Ex. 35 in combination with Ex. 36.

The recapitulation emerges quietly. The contrast of major

and minor in Ex. 35 is now reversed – minor leads to major – and the scoring is changed. There is some further variation in this section, which leads to a different version of the 'hesitant theme' from any of the four heard in the exposition: it is now in C major with a sustained countermelody for the cello. The theme is repeated in the same key, with the violin triplets. Development follows as before, leading to a third statement in G major. Having now reached once more the tonic key Schubert must have decided, quite reasonably, that a fourth statement would be excessive. The triplets take command and lead to a coda consisting of a reassertion of the ambiguous tonality of the opening. To criticise the exposition solely on the grounds of its length, or to maintain that the movement is ill-balanced because the development section is so much shorter, is pointless. Everything in such a case depends on how the material is used. What is wrong with the exposition is its obsession with the 'hesitant theme'. Though the scoring of each version is different, the theme itself is almost entirely unchanged. There is no reason why variations should not form part of a sonata movement, but they should offer something more than mere repetition. The fact that three of the versions in the exposition are in the same key tends to emphasise a monotony which is not entirely banished by the charm of the actual sound.

There is a good deal of repetition also in the slow movement. It begins in E minor with a long, elegiac melody for the cello which is one of Schubert's finest inventions. The mood so established is shattered by a wild section in G minor, with a progression that sounds odd because one does not actually hear the chord implied by the isolated notes on the violin and viola:

EX. 37

Contrast of this kind, which one finds also in the slow movements of Schubert's piano sonatas, is effective enough, though it is weakened to some extent by the very conventional transition between the two sections. But having made his gesture of revolt, Schubert proceeds to make it all over again a semitone lower, in F♯ minor, which involves an adjustment in the transposition of the first bar of Ex. 37, since violins cannot play low F♯. It is simpler to summarise the rest of the movement by tabulating the complete scheme, including what has already been discussed:

A: elegiac melody, E minor
B: wild outburst, (a) G minor, (b) F♯ minor
A: B minor
B: D minor, more agitated than before
C: transition or development (fragments of A), F♯ minor
A: E minor and E major alternately
Coda, based on A: E minor

The movement is thus a kind of rondo, with the principal theme occuring in more than one key; but it suffers from the fact that the two episodes (B) are virtually identical except in key, and that the first one is repeated. There is even a possibility that the ear will weary of the elegiac melody if Schubert's direction to repeat the second half of the opening section is observed. It is in fact a relief when the tune strays into E major in the course of its last appearance. The parts of this movement are excellent, but there is a lack of judgement in the way they are assembled.

There is some inconsistency also in the Scherzo. The Trio, in a slower tempo, is a genial *Ländler* and none the worse for that; but it seems a very odd companion for the main body of the movement, which is marked 'Allegro vivace' and has a strange ethereal lightness. This is one of Schubert's most original scherzos. It is mainly quiet, with occasional outbursts, and has a fluttering motion that recalls Mendelssohn. The texture is clear and the interchange of parts is exceptionally deft. It is a pity that Schubert did not write a Trio to match this nimble footing. A dance of peasants, however discreet and amiable. is not an ideal partner for the skipping of fairy folk. In a ballet the contrast would be acceptable, because the visual image would make it intelligible. In a concert piece the association is an anomaly.

The Finale is a dance of a rather different character from the one in the D minor Quartet. From the very opening, which finds it difficult to decide whether to be major or minor, the atmosphere is very much that of *opera buffa*, though with far more harmonic ingenuity and variety than one would expect to find in an Italian work of this period. The suggestion here is not of dancers absorbed in their occupation but rather of a number of people involved in a never-ending imbroglio. One could carry the analogy further and say that there are obviously villains on the stage but it is quite clear that they are not going to prevail. The very considerable length of this movement is a tribute not only to Schubert's staying power but also to the fertility of his invention. The structure is that of a rondo, with all kinds of quirks and modifications, but no one who listens to it is likely to be bothered by the way it is put together. One of the happiest details is the appearance in the development of a suave tune in C♯ minor which sounds new until one realises that it is a transformation and extension of a dancing figure in the exposition. It is impossible not to succumb to music which has so many surprises round the corner. The quartet as a whole is almost an epitome of Schubert's approach to instrumental music in its sudden flashes of insight, its melodic charm, its harmonic waywardness, its insistence on rhythm and its willingness to deviate when something inviting appears by the wayside.

STRING TRIOS

Schubert wrote two string trios, both in the key of B♭ major, D. 471 (1816) and 581 (1817). The first of these is incomplete, consisting only of a first movement and a fragmentary Andante: it is an innocent, unenterprising piece. The second is beautifully written for the instruments and includes a prominent part for the viola, which has the melody throughout the Trio of the Minuet:

this was the instrument that Schubert himself played in domestic music-making. Though there are incidental signs of the composer's individuality, the work as a whole is too much like an essay in eighteenth-century style to deserve more than a passing notice.

PIANO TRIOS

Considering that Schubert was a pianist and wrote so many works for his instrument, it is curious that he devoted so little attention to concerted music with piano. There are only five works for more than two instruments, and only three of these are of major importance: the Piano Quintet and the Piano Trios in B♭ major, Op. 99, D. 898, and E♭ major, Op. 100, D. 929. The Adagio and Rondo concertante in F major for piano, violin, viola and cello, D. 487 (1816), hardly comes into the category of chamber music: it is rather a miniature concerto, which, like other works of this period shows strongly the influence of eighteenth-century models. A single movement for piano trio in B♭ major, D. 28,[1] called 'Sonata' by the composer, survives from 1812. According to the manuscript it took over a month to write. Like the early quartets it shows that Schubert had still to learn how to organise a movement, though he was obviously familiar with the idioms of his predecessors. The Adagio for piano trio in E♭ major, D. 897, published as Op. 148 in 1845 under the title 'Nocturne', appears to date from 1826. If the theory is correct that it was originally intended as the slow movement of the Piano Trio in B♭ major, D. 898, one can only be thankful that Schubert rejected it. We know that 1826 was not a happy year for him. He was again in poor health, and his attempts to secure an official position had not been successful. It may well be that the Adagio is evidence that his imagination was temporarily the victim of his misfortunes.

The Piano Trio in E♭ major dates from 1827. The Piano Trio in B♭ major cannot have been written very much earlier, possibly in 1826, since Schubert called it Op. 99 and the E♭ major Op. 100. The B♭ major Trio was not published till 1836. The E♭ major Trio, which was performed at Schubert's concert in March 1828, was accepted by the publisher Probst of Leipzig, but there was

[1] Published by the Wiener Philharmonischer Verlag in 1923.

considerable delay over its appearance in print. As late as October 1828, just under seven weeks before he died, Schubert wrote impatiently to ask what was happening. Whether Probst actually got the work out before 19 November is uncertain; but there seems to be no record that Schubert ever saw a copy. Both trios have long been part of the staple fare of amateur ensembles; but both of them demand the highest professional standards of performance. The cello part, much of which is written in the higher part of the instrument's compass, is particularly demanding: but pianists also will recall a number of passages that require a good deal of private practice before they seem inevitable. Schubert was fortunate in having first-rate performers. In a letter dated 18 January 1828 he mentions a performance of 'a trio of mine for pianoforte, violin and violoncello' (presumably the one in E♭ major) which took place 'the other day': the performance was actually at the end of December 1827. The players were Carl Maria von Bocklet (piano), Ignaz Schuppanzigh (violin) and Joseph Linke, the cellist in Schuppanzigh's quartet. Some indication of Bocklet's playing can be guessed not only from the E♭ major Trio but also from the Piano Sonata in D major, D. 850 (1825), which was dedicated to him, and the very elaborate Fantasy for violin and piano in C major, D. 934 (1827). A good deal of the piano writing in the B♭ major Trio, and to a lesser degree in the E♭ major Trio, is in octaves, rather as if it were the upper part in a piano duet. This characteristic has been noted already in connection with the Piano Quintet. It is not altogether surprising, since Schubert liked playing piano duets and wrote several.

The first movement of the B♭ major Trio impresses by its buoyancy and its tremendous air of confidence. Whatever Schubert's troubles may have been in 1826 he managed in this work to thrust them behind him. The form of the movement is surprisingly simple: an exposition with only two principal keys and two themes, a reasonably short development which makes use of both these themes, a normal recapitulation and a very brief coda. However, there is one detail of the recapitulation which is original. After the dominant preparation at the end of the development, which seems to herald the return of the opening theme in B♭ major, there is a switch in the harmony and the theme reappears in G♭ major. It is then repeated in D♭ major and does not reach the tonic key until the piano takes it up. There is room here for analytical discussion. If you maintain that the beginning of a recapitulation is determined by the key, not by the theme, then it begins at the point where the piano has the theme. On the other hand, there are plenty of other examples in Schubert's works of recapitulations that do not begin in the tonic key. In any case the argument is purely academic, since what we hear in G♭ major is the return of the opening of the movement, and the fact that it is in the 'wrong' key, so far from being an obstacle, is an additional source of enjoyment. A good deal of musical analysis would be better if writers would use their ears instead of looking at the printed page.

The slow movement, which is relatively short, also has an ingenious system of key relationships. The structure is as follows:

First section   – A: E♭ major, modulating at the end to
                 B: B♭ major, returning at the end to E♭ major
Middle section – C: C minor, repeated in C major
Final section   – A: A♭ major, E major, C major
                 B: E♭ major

The theme of A, which in the final section changes key in midstream, is one of those slow-moving melodies of which Schubert was a master. Like so many of his instrumental themes it could be sung, and yet at the same time it is different in character from the melodies of his songs, because it is not tied to words and so has complete freedom of rhythm. The middle section is equally expressive but suffers a little from excessive decoration: the purpose may have been to provide a more decisive contrast to the first section, but it is noticeable that in slow movements Schubert is apt to give way to the temptation to add icing to the cake. In this instance the virtuosity of the performers he had in mind may have been an additional inducement. The decoration is abandoned abruptly as the final section begins; and here there is the additional pleasure of hearing the key change within the melody and not merely at its repetition.

The Scherzo in some ways recalls the Scherzo of the G major Quartet, though the material is quite different. It is so neat and light-fingered that it is irresistible, not only at a first hearing but for long afterwards. Here the piano makes a perfect foil to the

D

strings and the texture throughout is crystal clear. The Trio, with no change of tempo, is the ideal contrast: smooth sustained melodies for violin and cello with an accompaniment in waltz rhythm for the piano. The Finale, curiously described as a rondo, though the principal theme occurs only twice, inhabits a different world. It is also an unfortunate example of Schubert's tendency to go on at all costs. It is over 650 bars long and consists of an enormous exposition, the return of the principal theme, a perfunctory development, a recapitulation without the principal theme, and a short coda marked 'Presto'. The exposition covers a bewildering variety of keys. At the point where it has settled down firmly in F major, suggesting that the principal theme is going to recur, the music goes back on its tracks and embarks on a digression in Db major, based on a bold thematic fragment which is striking the first time it appears in G minor but far outstays its welcome. Eventually, in bar 281, the principal theme turns up in Eb major. The recapitulation takes us over much of the same ground as the exposition, though in different keys. The principal theme of the movement, if it can be called that, has the innocent gaiety that one finds in many of Schubert's finales; but there is so much emphasis on the subsidiary material that the innocent gaiety has disappeared long before the end and has given place to manufactured frivolity.

The Eb major Trio demands even more brilliance, if that is possible, than its predecessor. Once again the first movement opens with a bald statement; but this time it is not a swinging tune but rather a kind of motto that appears in various forms in what follows. The mood is short-lived. The key switches to B minor, in which we hear a cryptic utterance which has some affinity with the Minuet in the same key in the Piano Sonata in G major, D. 894 (1826):

EX. 38

This passes through other keys until Bb major is reached, with sinister echoes of a fragment from the opening statement. In this key occurs briefly a tranquil passage which is the second principal theme of the movement. It is quickly brushed aside and the exposition ends defiantly. But the tranquil theme comes into its own in the development, where it is accompanied by cascades of triplets from the piano, similar to those in the Impromptu in Ab major for piano solo, D. 899, No. 4 (1827). Schubert likes this so much that he repeats it at a higher level, and most of it for a third time in still another key. Only at the end of the development do we hear twice in the distance an echo of the motto, which leads to the recapitulation. It might be argued that the device of repeating a whole section of the development, which Schubert also did in the String Quintet, shows a lack of inventiveness. But since the exposition is marked to be repeated, as in most classical movements in sonata form, there seems no reason why there should not be repetition in the development, particularly if it is in a different key, though whether we want to hear it a third time is another matter. The movement as a whole is well constructed and economical in its use of thematic material. There is little suggestion of wandering here. Apart from the rare moments of tranquillity there is a continuous sense of movement – sometimes a jogging movement, as in Ex. 38 – towards a goal which has been foreseen.

The opening theme of the slow movement is said to be a Swedish air, entitled, according to Nottebohm, 'Se, solen sjunker' (See the sun is sinking). If these are the opening words of the song there must have been a an initial up-beat which Schubert has discarded. Leopold Sonnleithner, who was the first to mention the source of the tune, was writing several years later, and there is no reason to suppose that his memory was infallible. On the other hand the tune is not markedly Schubertian (though the contrary has been urged), and the story may be true. Unfortunately the song has not been discovered, so that even if it was the source of the tune we cannot say whether Schubert also borrowed the steady march-like tramp of the piano accompaniment, if indeed the song ever had one. The melody is first played by the cello:

EX. 39

The figures marked *a* and *b* are significant: both of them play an important part in the second section of the exposition and in the stormy development. The movement is a rondo, with the melody appearing for the third time in a shortened form and a slower tempo. In the closing bars violin and cello take a last look at figure *a*.

The Scherzo, in a moderate tempo, has the same lightness and clarity as the one in the B♭ major Trio. Most of it is in canon, or close imitation, between piano and strings. The Trio, on the other hand, is heavy-footed, like a clog dance of peasants, and is not distinguished by particularly original invention. The ingenuous opening of the Finale should not deceive the listener into thinking that this is going to be a short movement. Schubert's apparently innocent beginnings often turn out to be the signpost for a good deal of less innocent activity. This finale (in 6/8 time) is in fact considerably longer than the one in the B♭ major Trio, not merely because it runs to nearly 750 bars but because the tempo is more moderate. The exposition is again excessively long. The first section in E♭ major (6/8) comes to an abrupt stop. It is followed by a section in C minor (2/2), *pp*, with the violin and cello in turn playing what sounds like the strumming of a mandoline. The music then reverts to a boisterous 6/8 with a change to the key of B♭ major, which sounds as if it were going to be the end of the exposition; but just when it appears that we have reached the closing bars, we have another bout of strumming in C minor, which is characteristically repeated in C major. Since it is improbable that the exposition will end in this key we have another boisterous section in B♭ major, in which key it eventually stops at bar 230. The following is the scheme:

A: E♭ major, 6/8
B: (1) C minor, 2/2
    (2) B♭ major, 6/8, related rhythmically to A
    (3) C minor and C major, 2/2
    (4) B♭ major, 6/8, related rhythmically to A

The development occupies another 210 bars. Beginning in B minor it deals at first with the material of B (4). Into this key, with the 6/8 rhythm still maintained by the piano, steals the 'Swedish' air from the slow movement, played by the cello. A change of key to D minor brings back the strumming figure from the exposition, B (1 and 3), which is subsequently repeated in B minor and F major. By way of E♭ minor, B minor and B♭ major the music, using material from B (2 and 4), eventually reaches the recapitulation, which is almost as long as the exposition. It is followed by an extended coda, beginning in E minor and corresponding to the beginning of the development. The key is soon switched to E♭ minor, which allows the 'Swedish' air to reappear, again on the cello. The movement ends triumphantly, like an opera finale, with a conventional assertion of E♭ major, a key which has so often been forgotten in what has gone before. It is an elaborate and ingenious movement, and the reminiscence of the 'Swedish' air – a device which was to be used frequently by later composers – is as effective as it is original. But it may be questioned whether the excessive repetition, particularly of the strumming figure, does not defeat its own object, and whether the constant changing of key does not tend to destroy any firm sense of tonality. The delights of this movement are in its incidents, but the incidents do not add up to a convincing whole.

WORKS FOR PIANO AND ONE OTHER INSTRUMENT

Schubert wrote six works for violin and piano: four sonatas (D major, D. 384, A minor, D. 385, G minor, D. 408, and A major, D. 574), a *Rondeau brilliant* in B minor, D. 895, and a Fantasy in C major, D. 934. The first three sonatas, dating from 1816, were published as 'Sonatinas', Op. 137, in 1836, though Schubert called them sonatas. The fourth sonata, composed in 1817, was published fifteen years later, entitled 'Duo', Op. 162. The Op. 137 sonatas share an admiration for Mozart which more than once trembles on the verge of reminiscence. In the first movement of the D major the principal theme is subjected to a development very similar to Ex. 17, p. 26, the origins of which can hardly be said to be obscure. The music is so clearly written and so agreeable to play that it seems almost churlish to say that not one of the three sonatas leaves any strong impression on the mind. Apart from the frequent changes of key there is hardly anything that would strike us at a first hearing as Schubertian.

The fourth sonata, in A major, illustrates Schubert's habit of using more than two keys in an exposition and also his inclination to desert the principal key of a movement at an early stage. The first movement settles happily in E major, only to change this to E minor. From there, by way of G major and a characteristic modulation to B major:

EX. 40

the music eventually comes back to E major again. In the slow movement, in C major, the principal key is abandoned after the first eight bars: a section in Db major follows before the original key returns. In the recapitulation there is a favourite device: the simple theme is accompanied by a rhythmical figure which is derived from the middle section of the movement. In this work the Scherzo precedes the slow movement, which is just as well, since the Finale has many of the characteristics of a scherzo. The work is grateful to play for both participants, but the melodic invention is not on the whole distinguished.

The *Rondeau brilliant* (1826) and the Fantasy in C major (1827) are both show pieces, written for the Czech violinist Josef Slavík, who was described by Chopin as a second Paganini. The *Rondeau*, which was published in 1827, is a powerful, extrovert work, with a bewildering variety of key changes and a long development section based on new material. The introductory Andante is linked with the Allegro not only by the fact that it provides the initial thematic impetus for the Rondo but also by the inclusion of some of its material at the end of the exposition. The Fantasy is a long and elaborate composition in several sections:

    I Andante molto (C major)
   II Allegretto (A minor and major, modulating to A♭ major)
 III Andantino (theme and variations, A♭ major)
 IV Tempo primo (modified recapitulation of I, C major)
  V Allegro vivace (C major and A major)
 VI Allegretto (further variation of III, A♭ major)
VII Presto (coda of V, C major)

When it was first performed by Slavík and Bocklet in January 1828 a Viennese critic wrote:

The Fantasy occupied rather too much of the time a Viennese is prepared to devote to pleasures of the mind. The hall emptied gradually, and the writer confesses that he too is unable to say anything about the conclusion of this piece of music.

This must be almost the only occasion on which a music critic has admitted that he left before a piece was finished. It is a pity he did not stay to the end, as the final coda is a brilliant piece of writing, which may even make one forget the inequality of what has gone before.

There is nothing wrong with the structure of the work, which is ingenious and convincing; and the opening Andante molto, though it imposes on the pianist the labour of playing *tremolando pianissimo,* offers the violinist every opportunity for displaying a warm, lyrical tone. Unfortunately the other opportunities for display are of a more mundane kind. Conscious that he could rely on two outstanding virtuosos Schubert wrote a work designed to dazzle the audience. Supreme virtuosity might bring the work off at the present day; but anything less exposes the hollowness of much of the invention, even though the jaunty Hungarian idioms of section II fall easily on the ear. In section III Schubert used a theme derived from his song 'Sei mir gegrüsst' (Receive my greetings), D. 741 (1821). Instead of taking over the vocal melody he produced a new composite version, based partly on the tune and partly on the piano accompaniment, and dressed it up with rather sickly harmonies. There was nothing much to be done with a theme of this character. All that Schubert offers is a series of extravaganzas which test the ability of the players but reduce the audience to the condition of spectators watching performing seals at a circus.

Even when he was unwell and occupied with the music he wanted to write, Schubert seems to have been willing to respond to requests from his friends. In 1824, the year of the quartets in A minor and D minor and the 'Grand Duo' for piano duet, he somehow found time to write not only the Octet for Count von Troyer but also the Sonata in A minor for arpeggione and piano, D. 821, and the Introduction and Variations in E minor for flute and piano, D. 802. The sonata was written for Vincenz Schuster, a guitar-player who was among those taking part in the regular music-making at the Sonnleithner house. The arpeggione was a hybrid instrument which had been invented in the previous year by Georg Staufer, who called it the guitar-cello. Like a guitar it had six strings and frets on the finger-board, but it was bowed like a cello. Schuster seems to have been the chief exponent of the instrument, since he wrote a method for it which was published in 1825. Its life was short and undistinguished, and if it were not for Schubert's sonata it would be known today only as an entry in a catalogue of musical instruments. The invitation to write the work did not result in anything as stimulating as the Octet. Nor does Schubert seem to have been interested in the individual characteristics of the instrument. There are a few thrummed chords in the first movement, and a couple of bowed chords at the end of this movement and at the end of the Finale;

but otherwise most of the music might have been written for a normal string instrument, and in fact it is generally played on the cello at the present day, though this presents some problems in the higher register, since the top string of the arpeggione was E above middle C, a fifth higher than the cello's A string.

The sonata is not negligible: it is written, as one might expect, with complete professional assurance. But there is a lack of involvement, and Schubert's mannerisms, which in other works so often spark off new ideas, seem here rather like spare parts which are fitted into the music at the expected places without contributing anything vital to its progress. The most appealing movement is the Adagio in E major. Here we have a rare example of a melody that might have come from one of Schubert's songs. It is simple rather than eloquent, but its very simplicity is striking after some of the conventional junketing of the first movement. Unfortunately Schubert seems to have been content to be not only simple but brief. The Adagio turns out to be little more than an introduction to the final Allegretto, into which it leads. There was material here for a movement that might have stood comparison with the slow movement of the String Quintet; but perhaps Schubert was in a hurry, or not in the mood.

The other work of 1824, the Introduction and Variations in E minor, was written for Schubert's close friend Ferdinand Bogner, who on the evidence of this piece must have been an unusually accomplished flautist. The theme of the variations is once again adapted from one of Schubert's own songs: 'Trock'ne Blumen' (Withered flowers), from the song cycle *Die schöne Müllerin*, D. 795 (1823). This pathetic little song is not unsuitable for variations, provided they respect the character of the theme. Schubert, however, seems to have been quite indifferent to the implications of his own music. His concern here, as in the C major Fantasy for violin and piano, was to provide material for the exercise of virtuosity. That he has done this is undeniable. Not only the flautist but the pianist as well are put through their paces. If anything, the piano part is more demanding than the flautist's: a player whose left hand is not athletic enough to cope with rapid octaves had better leave the work alone. But the total effect of this series of escapades is depressing; and when the variations eventually issue into a march of quite remarkable vulgarity one is constrained to cry 'Enough'. The work might conceivably be tolerable if it were particularly well written for the flute; but it is not.

There are people who are temperamentally allergic to Schubert's music and find it difficult to understand why others admire it. On the other hand there are Schubertians so devout that they regard any criticism of their idol as akin to blasphemy. The truth, naturally enough, lies between these extremes. There is inferior music in Schubert, as there is in Mozart and Beethoven. We judge composers of this calibre by their greatest achievements and are possibly inclined to be more severe on their lapses than we should be in the case of second-rate men. In Schubert there is the further difficulty that his less happy ideas are apt to occur side by side with others which are sublime. The reason lies partly in his environment and partly in himself. He lived among people who were passionately devoted to making music, and for them he wrote a good deal of music which at its best is charming and at its worst is trivial. He was also so obsessed with the necessity of creating that he does not always seem to have had time to reflect whether what he was writing was appropriate to its context.

It is not true that he poured his ideas on paper without previous cogitation. Like other composers he made sketches, and would modify these when it came to the finished work. The piano draft of the 'Unfinished' Symphony is illuminating as an example of first thoughts which were altered at a later stage. Sometimes too, he was plainly dissatisfied with what he had written and left works unfinished. But once a work was finished he seems to have been content;[1] the alteration which he made in the principal theme of the first movement of the C major Symphony is an unusual example of a correction carried out after the score was complete. According to Anton Schindler, Schubert once spent a long time examining the autograph score of Beethoven's *Fidelio*. When he had finished he declared that he could not understand why the composer had made so many alterations: he thought the original ideas were just as good as the improvements and said that he personally had no time for corrections of this kind. The point is

[1] This applies to his instrumental works. A number of his early songs exist in several versions.

mentioned by his friend Josef von Spaun, who wrote in 1864:

There is one fault with which Schubert can be reproached and it is that he never took his compositions in hand again and polished them, with the result that tedious passages or inaccuracies occur here and there; but the question is whether that really was a fault and whether the freshness and originality of his compositions due to this do not far outweigh the lack of polishing.

This is a shrewd comment, though it is not clear what is meant by 'inaccuracies'. Spaun was probably right in saying that if Schubert had revised his works there would have been a loss of spontaneity; and spontaneity is one of the characteristics to which his music owes much of its appeal. But it may be questioned whether the considerable amount of repetition to be found in the G major Quartet, the String Quintet and the two piano Trios does not exceed the limits of spontaneity. Schubert so often showed a remarkable flair for developing and transforming his initial ideas that it seems strange that on occasion he was willing merely to repeat material with no significant change other than that of key. One has the feeling that he was at times almost intoxicated by his own exuberance, and intoxication is not the ideal state of mind for self-criticism. One finds also in his serious works the acceptance of ideas which would be very happy in a *divertimento* or in music for a private party but which have a slightly incongruous air in their immediate surroundings. The finales of the A minor Quartet and the String Quintet seem to drag us too rudely from the atmosphere established by the preceding movements. Clearly Schubert was not conscious of any incongruity. For him music did not exist in separate compartments; and if his inclination to gaiety took him in the direction of café music or street songs he saw no reason to shackle it.

It is hardly necessary to say that he had a unique gift for melody: his songs are the best evidence. It is significant that all the melodies in his instrumental works are singable, even though they may exceed the compass of the human voice. But the relation between his songs and his instrumental works is not quite so simple as is sometimes supposed. Apart from the occasions when he used a song as a theme for variations, his instrumental melodies are normally not song tunes played by a violin or a cello. They have a life and character of their own, which seems to arise from the very nature of the chosen instrument. Schubert wrote superbly for string instruments, except possibly the arpeggione, because he himself had been a string-player from childhood and had the instinct to give them melodies that can truthfully be said to 'sing'. When, in the trios and the Piano Quintet, he transferred these melodies to the piano, the result was less happy, largely, one imagines, because in the excitement of invention he had not realised that a keyboard instrument is incapable of carrying the listener forward with sustained tone. His writing for the piano in general is often curiously unidiomatic, except where he is using it for accompaniment. In the songs and in the violin sonatas it is an effective partner to the soloists. But much of the writing in the piano sonatas is either orchestral in texture or, so to speak, neutral – music for an instrument but not specifically designed for the piano. In the trios and the Piano Quintet the practice of writing for the piano as if it were the *primo* part of a duet may be temporarily effective; but as a consistent device it is not the best way of combining string and keyboard instruments.

There is another type of thematic invention in Schubert's instrumental works which has nothing to do with melody. It consists of what might be called a neutral statement which is not of prime significance in itself but is seen to be so at a later stage. Both the D minor and the G major quartets open in this way, in marked contrast to the A minor, which accepts a flowing melody from the outset. The Eb major Trio also has a neutral, though assertive, opening; but in this case very little is made of it in the course of the movement. Examples in the piano sonatas are numerous. Sometimes the neutral opening almost makes us feel as though we had come in during the course of a conversation, the drift of which will not be apparent until later. Though such openings may not be melodic in the accepted sense, they always have very marked rhythmical features. Rhythm of all kinds is one of the strongest weapons in Schubert's armoury. Sometimes it develops mannerisms, like the marching dactyls to which reference has already been made, or the little curling up-beat figure, rising or falling, with which he likes to begin a scherzo. But these mannerisms are not tiresome, any more than the familiar gestures of someone we know well; and they are only a part of the tireless rhythmical energy which makes even a slow movement sound as if it were moving forward inevitably to a predetermined end. It is the rhythms that make tolerable the repetitions and the digressions – at least for anyone who will allow them to confound his judgement. It is the rhythms, too, that are half the charm of those Schubertian melodies that everyone knows and whistles.

It would be a mistake to say that there are no secrets in Schubert's music. But his mature chamber works do not, like Beethoven's, inhabit a private world of their own. There is suffering but not frustration. Hearing any one of these works we can imagine ourselves looking into the work-room where he composed ceaselessly up till two o'clock in the afternoon. At his desk he was committed. After that came the coffee house, a walk, the theatre or a party with friends. The afternoon and evening may very well have sown ideas in his head; but he was not the slave of his invention, he was not tormented by the fact that life is short – how short he was fortunate not to know. Whatever misfortunes and setbacks he had, he was at heart a happy man. We know that from his friends: we can tell it also from the music, which has brought happiness in turn to many who are blissfully unaware of the skill and science that have gone into its creation.

[1] G.A.=*Gesamtausgabe* (Complete Edition), published by Breitkopf & Härtel, Leipzig (reprint by Dover, New York).

[2] Rev.=*Revisionsbericht* (Critical Report) to the *Gesamtausgabe*.

[3] Only two movements in G.A. First complete edition, ed. by Maurice Brown (Breitkopf & Härtel, Wiesbaden, 1956).

[4] Ed. by Alfred Orel (Universal Edition, Vienna, 1939).

[5] Ed. by Alfred Orel (Wiener Philharmonischer Verlag, Vienna, 1923).
[6] Incomplete edition. First complete edition in G.A.